Bible Verses in Nature

Bear Creek Park

The photos in this book were taken on my many visits to Bear Creek Park in Keller, TX. The park is a wonderful blend of nature with a myriad of God's creatures milling, playing, foraging and living in the trees and creek itself. Mix in the people who gather to fish or enjoy its walking trails, pickleball courts, sports fields, playgrounds, and picnic areas and you have an area where humans and animals can thrive in a calm, tranquil setting amidst a bustling city environment that too often ties us to the man-made trappings of life.

I began visiting the park to write poetry and study for the various courses I was enrolled in at St. Elizabeth Ann Seton Catholic church, located just a couple of miles down the road. These visits evolved into walking the main trail loop before or after work, where I would encounter squirrels, ducks, birds, and turtles performing their daily routines. It was during these walks that I had the idea to take photographs and construct a book with accompanying bible verses. Over the next several months, I took hundreds of pictures, and combed through the bible, looking for verses that I felt would be both inspiring and tell a relatable story for the image.

I hope you enjoy this collection and remember to visit your local parks or nature preserves to get closer to God in nature.

1 Timothy 5:8

And whoever does not provide for family members, has denied the faith and is worse than an unbeliever.

Jeremiah 5:21,23

Hear this, O foolish and senseless people, who have eyes, but do not see, who have ears, but do not hear...but this people has a stubborn and rebellious heart; they have turned aside and gone away.

Ecclesiastes 4:9-10

Two are better than one, because they have a good reward for their toil. For if they fall, one will lift up the other; but woe to one who is alone and falls and does not have another to help.

Isaiah 6:8

Then I heard the voice of the Lord saying, 'Whom shall I send, and who will go for us?' and I said, 'Here I am; send me!'

Ecclesiastes 9:7

Go, eat your bread with enjoyment, and drink your wine with a merry heart; for God has long ago approved what you do.

Matthew 6:33

But first seek for the kingdom of God and his righteousness, and all these things will be given to you as well.

Matthew 18:20

For where two or more are gathered in my name, I am among them.

John 7:38

As the scripture has said, "Out of the believers heart shall flow rivers of flowing water."

Psalm 18:16

He reached down from on high, he took me; he drew me out of mighty waters.

Proverbs 3:5-6

Trust in the Lord with all your heart, and do not rely on your own insight.
In all your ways acknowledge him, and he will make straight your paths.

1Corinthians 13:12

For now we see in a mirror dimly, but then we will see face to face. Now I know only in part; then I will know fully, even as I have been fully known.

1 Corinthians 12:4-6

Now there are varieties of gifts, but the same Spirit; and there are varieties of services, but the same Lord; and there are varieties of activities, but it is the same God who activates all of them in everyone.

Matthew 11:28-30

Come to me, all you that are weary and are carrying heavy burdens, and I will give you rest. Take my yoke upon you, and learn from me; for I am gentle and humble in heart, and you will find rest for your souls. For my yoke is easy, and my burden is light.

Micah 7:7

But as for me, I will look to the Lord, I will wait for the God of my salvation; my God will hear me.

Proverbs 18:10

The name of the Lord is a strong tower; the righteous run into it and are safe.

Isaiah 43:2

When you pass through the waters,
I will be with you; and through the
rivers; they shall not overwhelm
you; when you walk through fire
you shall not be burned, and the
flame shall not consume you.

Philippians 3:13

Beloved, I do not consider that I have made it on my own; but this one thing I do: forgetting what lies behind and straining forward to what lies ahead, I press on towards the goal, for the prize of the heavenly call of God in Christ Jesus.

Ecclesiastes 4:12

And though one might prevail against another, two will withstand one. A threefold cord is not quickly broken.

Jeremiah 17:7-8

Blessed are those who trust in the Lord, whose trust is in the Lord. They shall be like a tree planted by water, sending out its roots by the stream. It shall not fear when heat comes, and its leaves shall stay green; in the year of drought it is not anxious, and it does not cease to bear fruit.

Revelation 22:1-2

Then the angel showed me the river of the water of life, bright as crystal, flowing from the throne of God and of the Lamb through the middle of the street of the city. On either side of the river is the tree of life with its twelve kinds of fruit, producing fruit for each month; and the leaves of the tree are for the healing of the nations.

Romans 12:2

Do not be conformed to this world, but be transformed by the renewing of your minds, so that you may discern what is the will of God – what is good and acceptable and perfect.

Daniel 4:10-11

Upon my bed this is what I saw; there was a tree at the center of the earth, and its height was great. The tree grew great and strong, its top reached to heaven, and it was visible to the ends of the whole earth. Its foliage was beautiful, its fruit abundant, and it provided food for all. The animals found shade under it, the birds of the air nested in its branches, and from it all living beings were fed.

Psalm 102:2

Do not hide your face from me in
the day of distress!
Incline your ear to me; answer me
speedily in the day I call.

Proverbs 6:7-8

Without having any chief or officer or ruler, it prepares its food in summer, and gathers its sustenance in harvest.

Proverbs 18:22

He who finds a wife finds a good thing, and obtains favor from the Lord.

Romans 12:16

Live in harmony with one another;
do not be haughty, but associate
with the lowly; do not claim to be
wiser than you are.

Philippians 2:3-4

Do nothing from selfish ambition or conceit, but in humility regard others as better than yourselves. Let each of you look not to your own interests, but to the interests of others.

Psalm 113:3

From the rising of the sun to its setting, the name of the Lord is to be praised.

Jeremiah 8:7

Even the stork in the heavens knows its times; and the turtle-dove, swallow and crane observe the time of their coming; but my people do not know the ordinance of the Lord.

1 Corinthians 15:58

Therefore, my beloved, be steadfast, immovable, always excelling in the work of the lord, because you know that in the Lord your labor is not in vain.

Psalm 104:19

You have made the moon to mark the seasons; the sun knows its time for setting.

Matthew 7:17-18

You will know them by their fruits. Are grapes gathered from thorns, or figs from thistles? In the same way, every good tree bears good fruit, but the bad tree bears bad fruit.

Genesis 1:9

Out of the ground the Lord God made to grow every tree that is pleasant to the sight and is good for food, the tree of life also in the midst of the garden, and the tree of the knowledge of good and evil.

Wisdom of Sirach 5:1-2

Do not be preoccupied by your wealth or say, 'I am self-sufficient'. Do not follow your inclination and strength, walking according to the desires of your heart.

Mark 9:42

If any of you put a stumbling block before one of these little ones who believe in me, it would be better for you if a great millstone were hung around your neck and you were thrown into the sea.

Matthew 6:26

Look at the birds of the air; they neither sow or reap nor gather into barns, and yet your heavenly Father feeds them. Are you not of more value than they?

Galatians 6:9

*So let us not grow weary in doing
what is right, for we will reap at
harvest time, if we do not give up.*

Psalm 27:8

'Come', my heart says, 'seek his face!' Your face Lord, do I seek. Do not hide your face from me.

Psalm 3:3

But you, O Lord, are a shield
around me, my glory, and the one
who lifts up my head. I cry aloud
to the Lord, and he answers me
from his holy hill.

John 7:37

On the last day of the festival, the great day, while Jesus was standing there, he cried out, 'Let anyone who is thirsty come to me, and let the one who believes in me drink.'

Jeremiah 23:24

Who can hide in secret places so that I cannot see them? says the Lord. Do I not fill heaven and earth, says the Lord?

Matthew 21:22

Whatever you ask for in prayer in
faith, you will receive.

Mark 1:12-13

And the spirit immediately drove him out into the wilderness. He was in the wilderness for forty days, tempted by Satan; and he was with the wild beasts; and the angels waited on him.

Romans 13:12

The night is far gone, the day is near. Let us then lay aside the works of darkness and put on the armour of light.

Genesis 8:22

As long as the earth endures, seedtime and harvest, cold and heat, summer and winter, day and night, shall not cease.

Psalm 139:9

If I take the wings of the morning and settle at the farthest limits of the sea, even there your hand shall lead me, and your right hand shall hold me fast.

Proverbs 17:14

The beginning of strife is like letting out water; so stop before the quarrel breaks out.

Sirach 51:11

I will praise your name continually, and will sing hymns of thanksgiving.

Deuteronomy 31:8

It is the Lord who goes before you. He will be with you; he will not leave you or forsake you. Do not fear or be dismayed.

Matthew 18:19

Again I say to you, if two of you agree on earth about anything they ask, it will be done for them by my Father in heaven.

Luke 21:27-28

And then they will see the Son of Man coming in a cloud with power and great glory. Now when these things begin to take place, straighten up and raise your heads, because your redemption is drawing near.

Job 12:7-9

'But ask the beasts, and they will teach you; the birds of the heavens, and they will tell you; or the bushes of the earth, and they will teach you; and the fish of the sea will declare it to you". Who among all these does not know that the hand of the Lord has done this?

Genesis 1:29

And God said, 'Behold, I have given you every plant yielding seed that is on the face of the earth, and every tree with seed in its fruit. You shall have them for food.

About the Author

Andrew W. Bauman is a Sacred Life Coach, working with people who want to improve their relationship with God, themselves, family, friends, or spouses. He is the author of two poetry books; *Born With Wings* and *Forest of Doubt* and writes a weekly poetry column for The Western Times newspaper, distributed in western Kansas.

Visit awbauman.com or scan the QR code to learn more.